Making a dinosaur

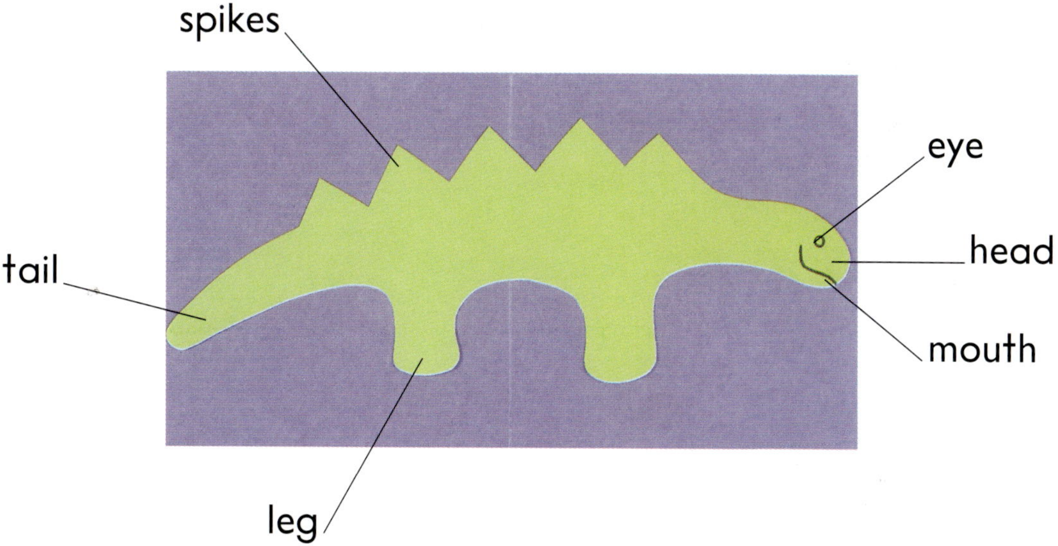

Look at the dinosaur.

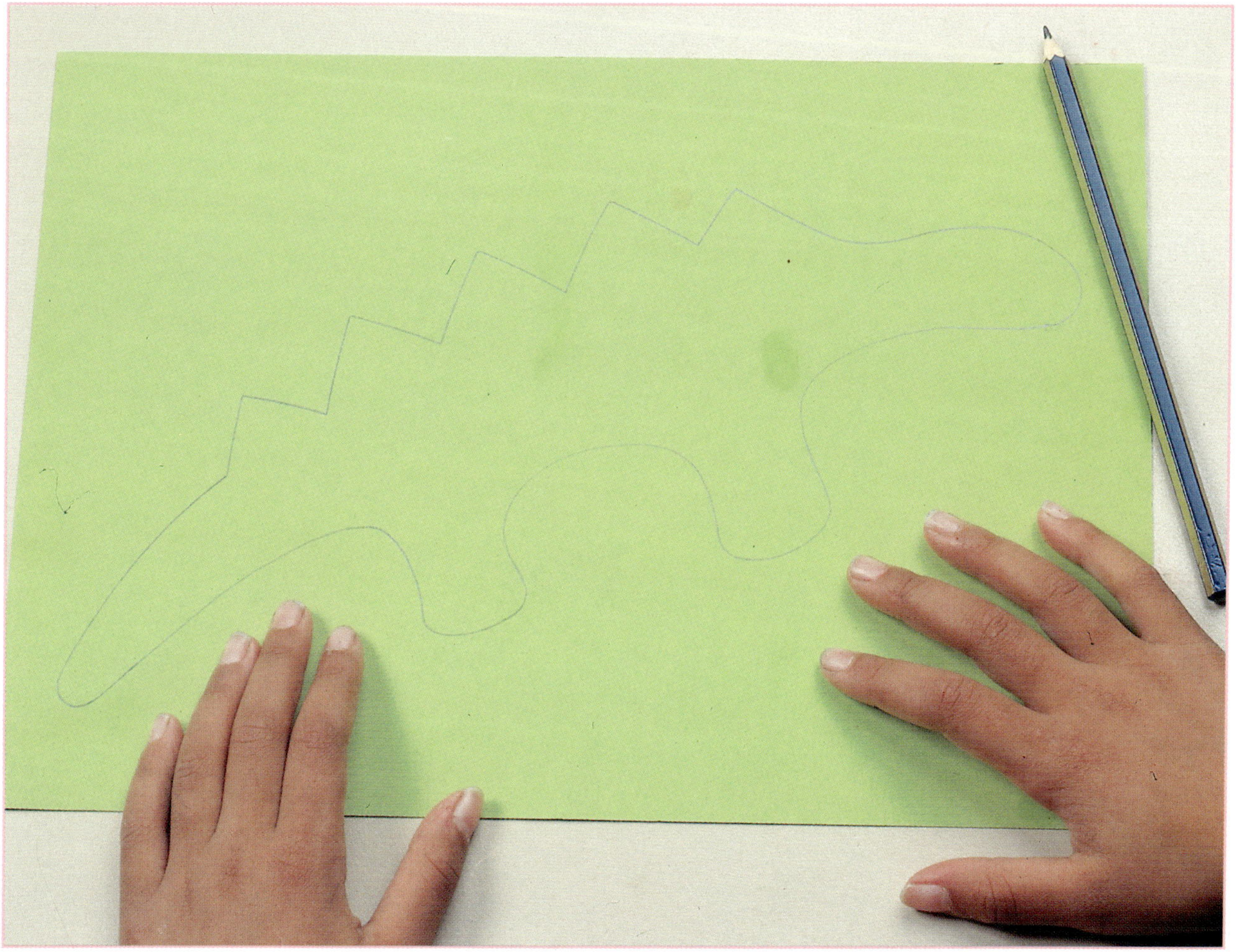

Look at the head.

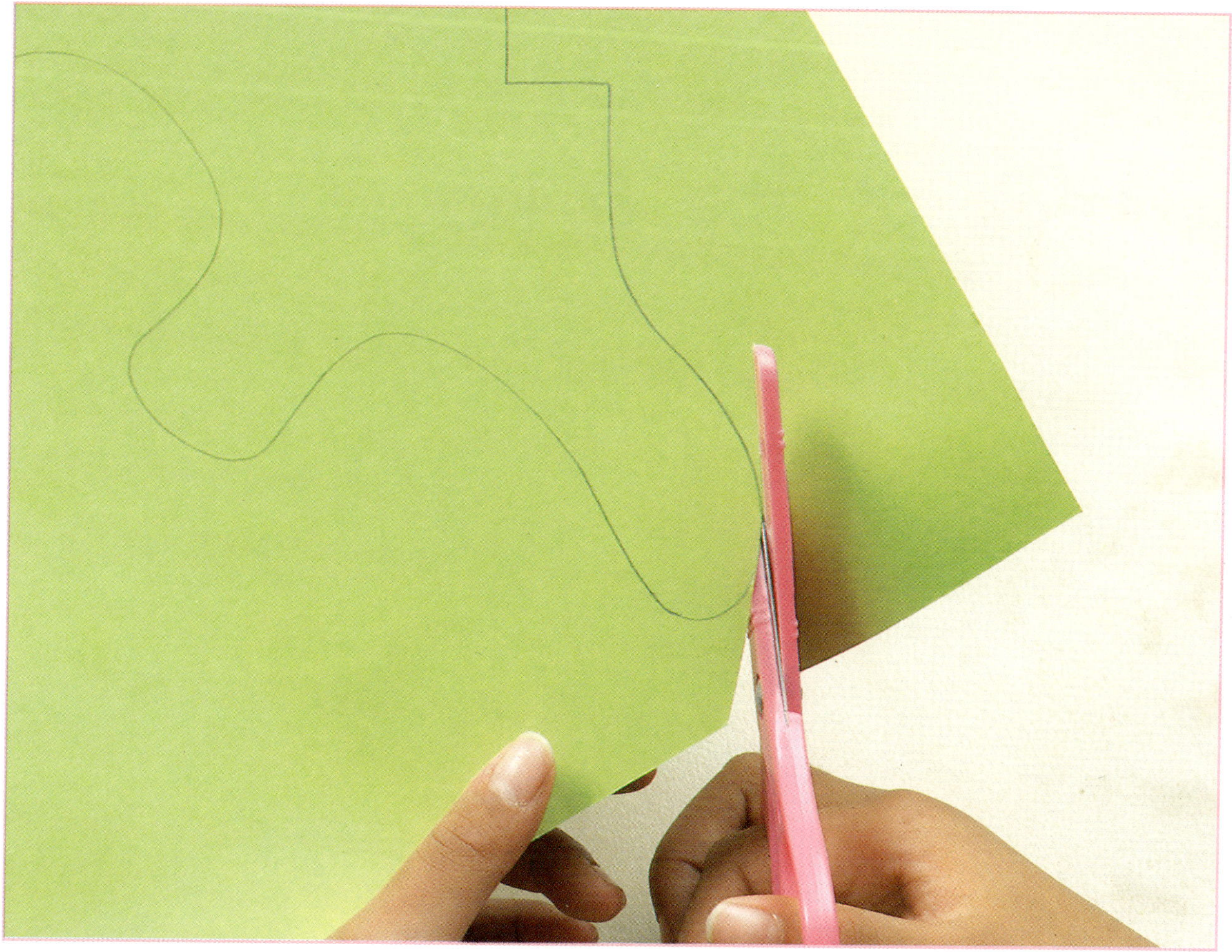

Look at the spikes.

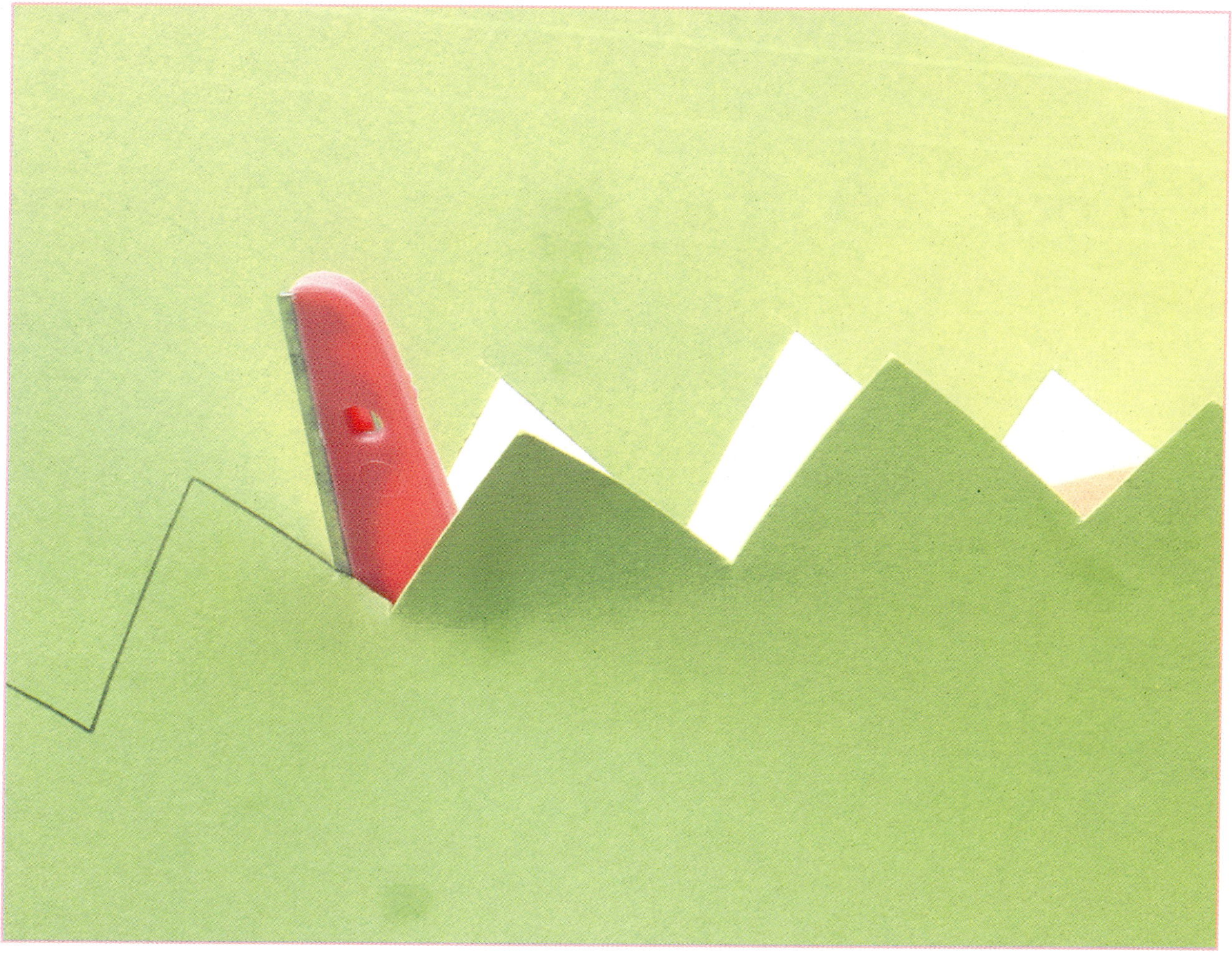

Look at the tail.

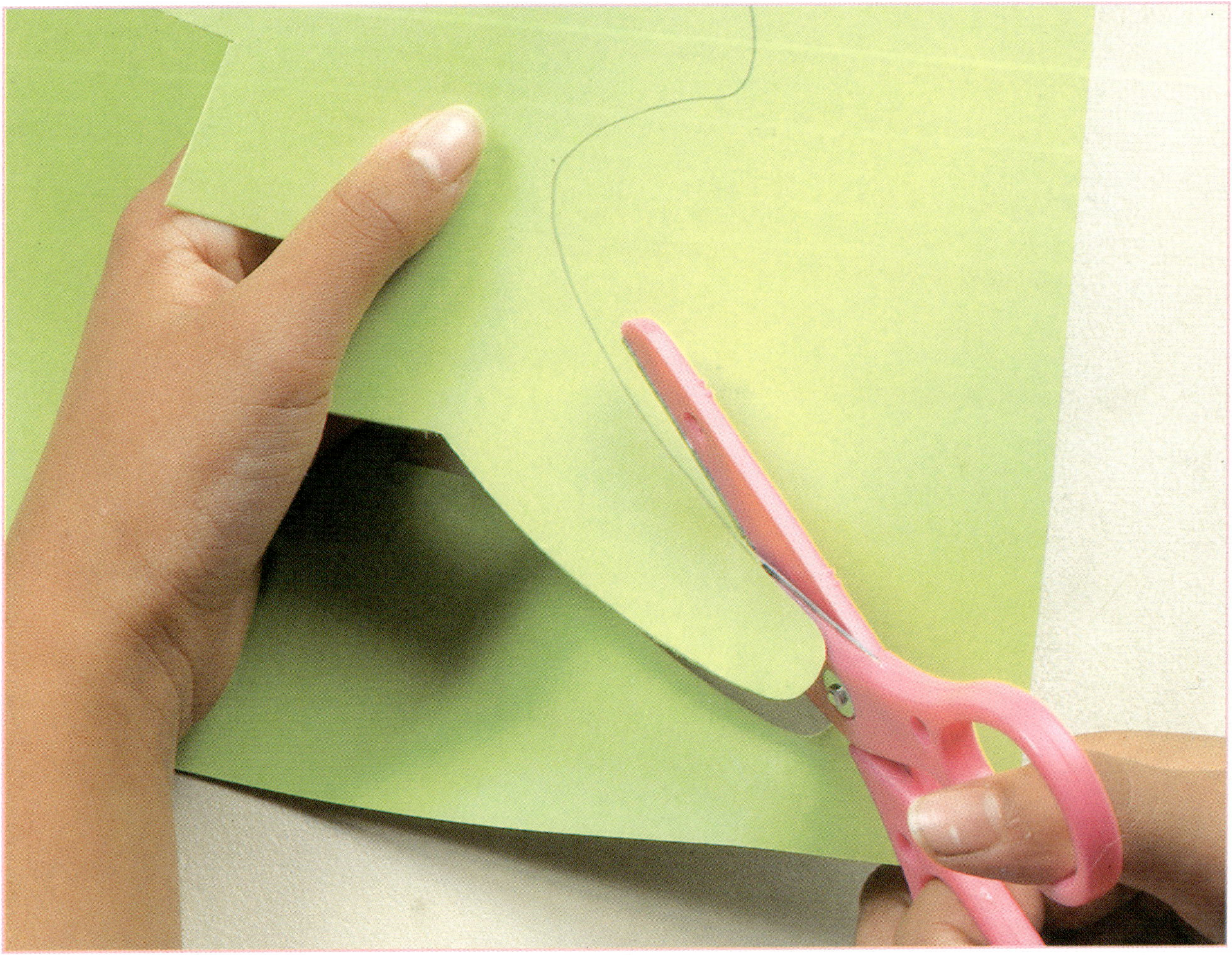

Look at the legs.

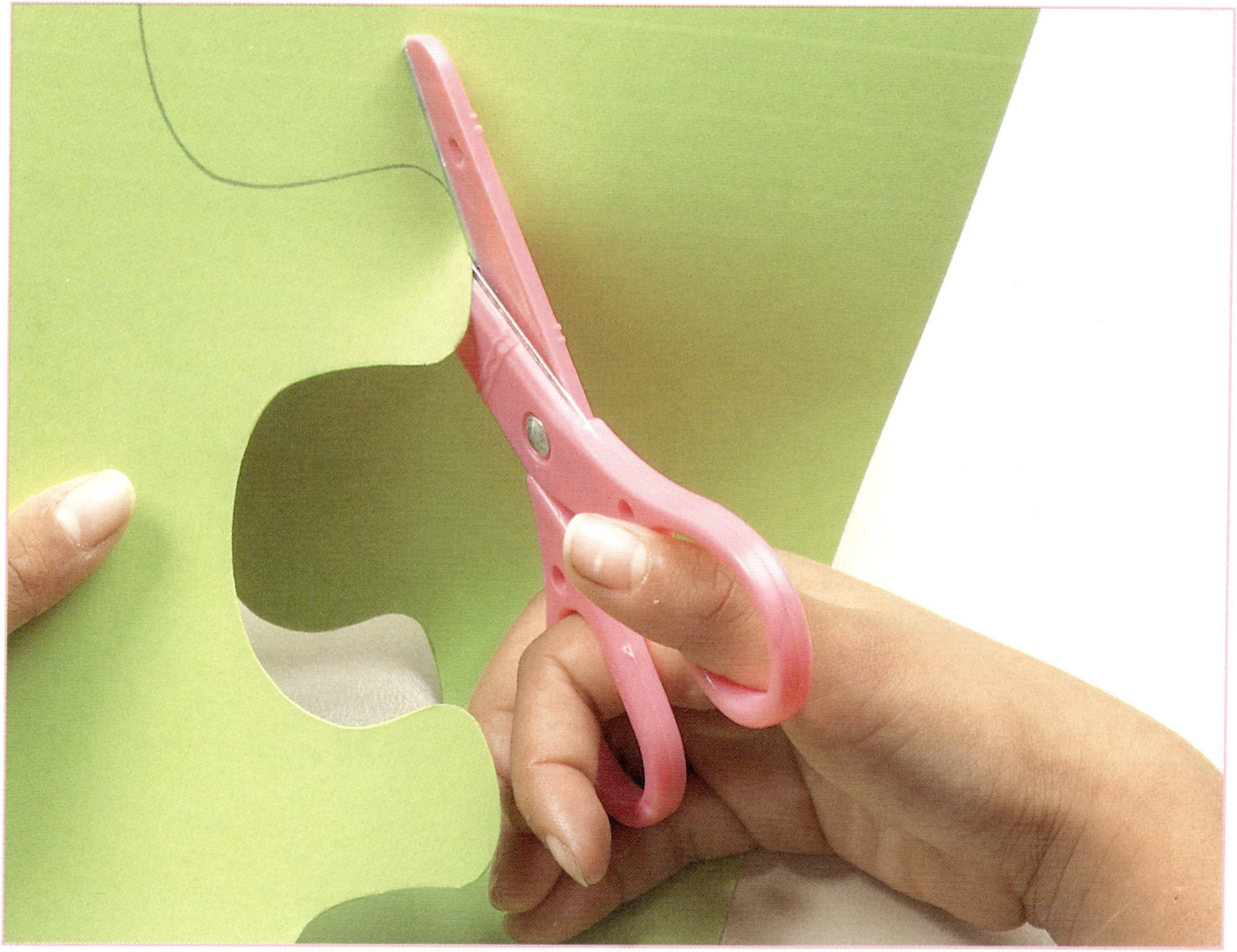

Look at the eye.

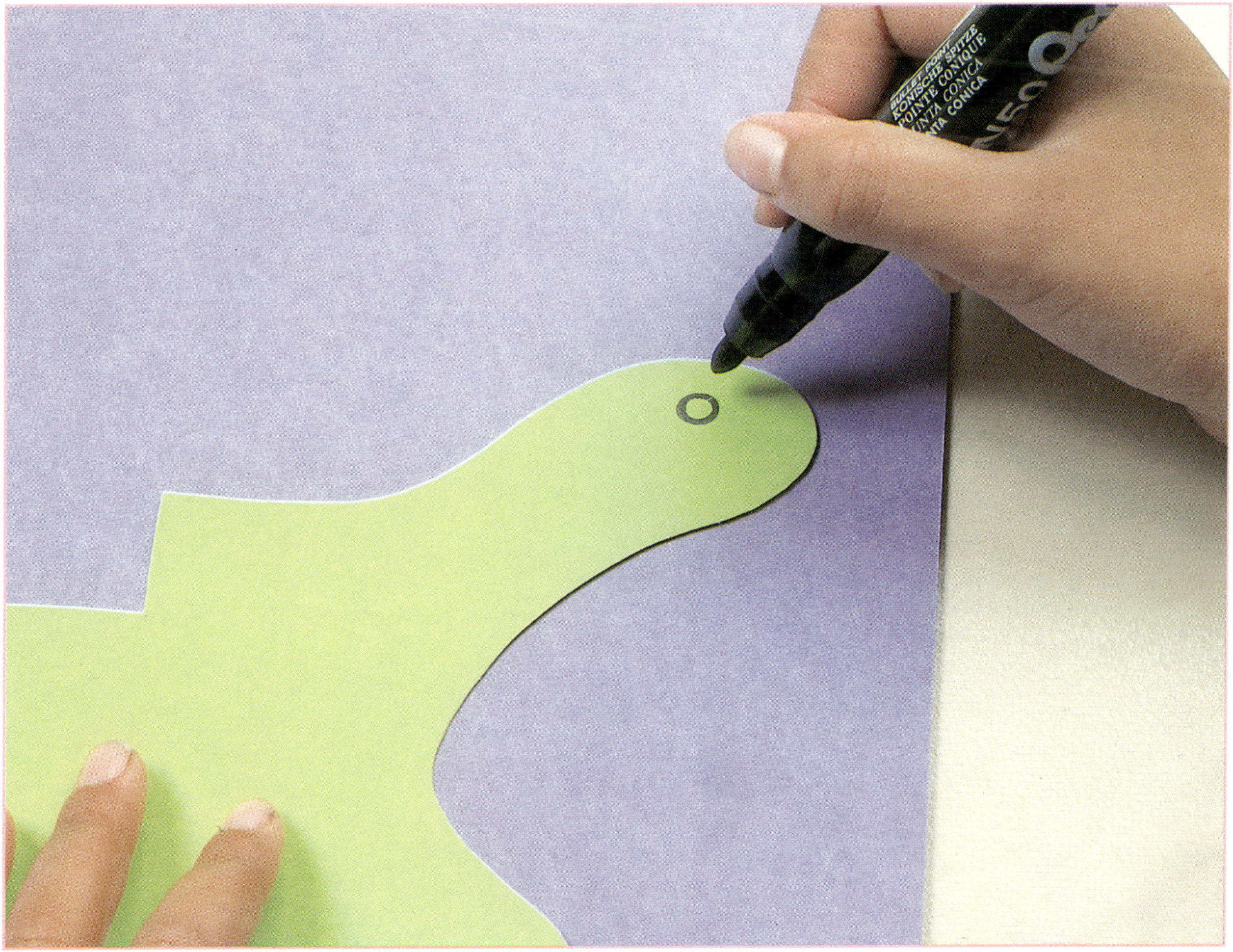
BULLET POINT
KONISCHE SPITZE
POINTE CONIQUE
PUNTA CONICA

Look at the mouth.

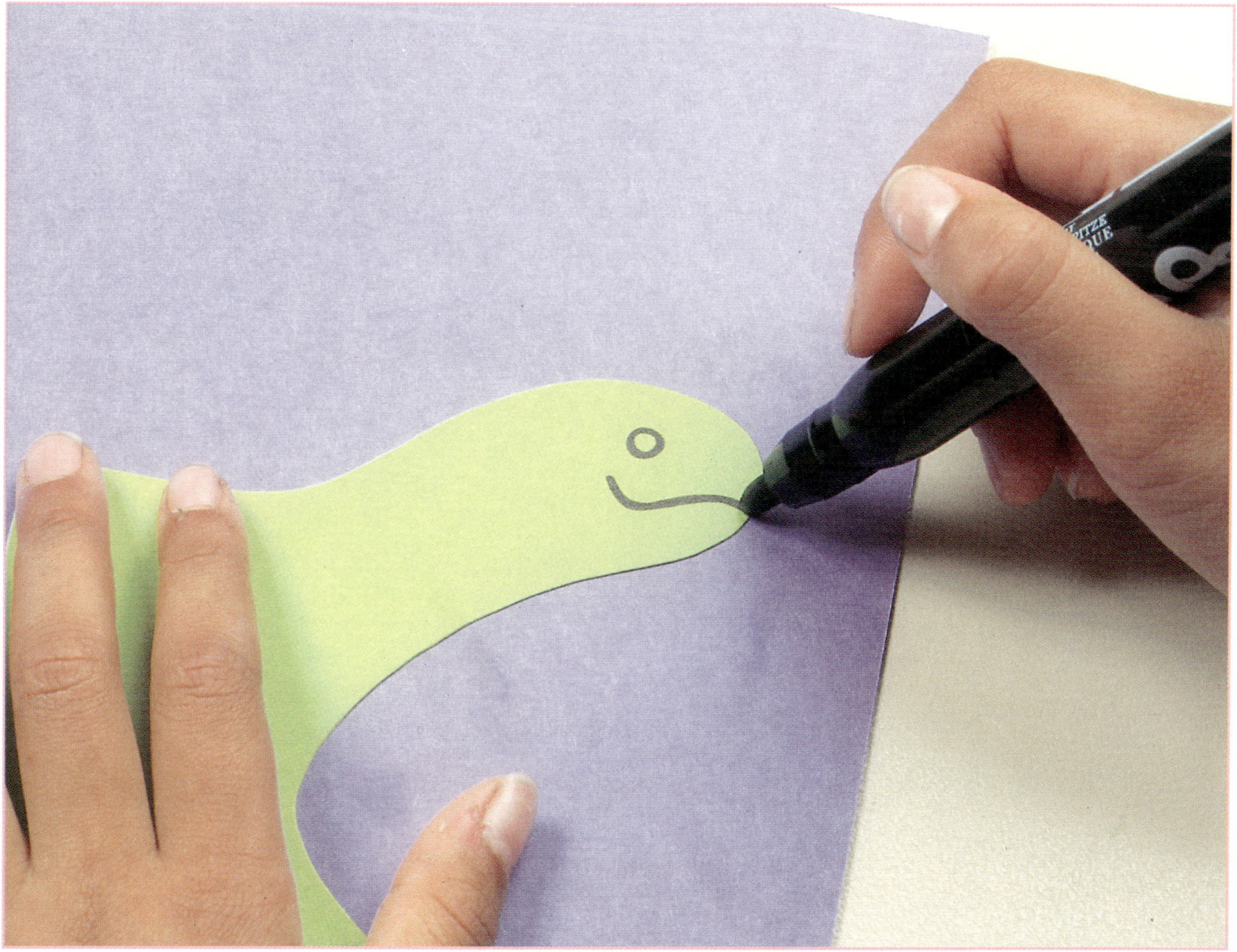

Here comes the dinosaur.

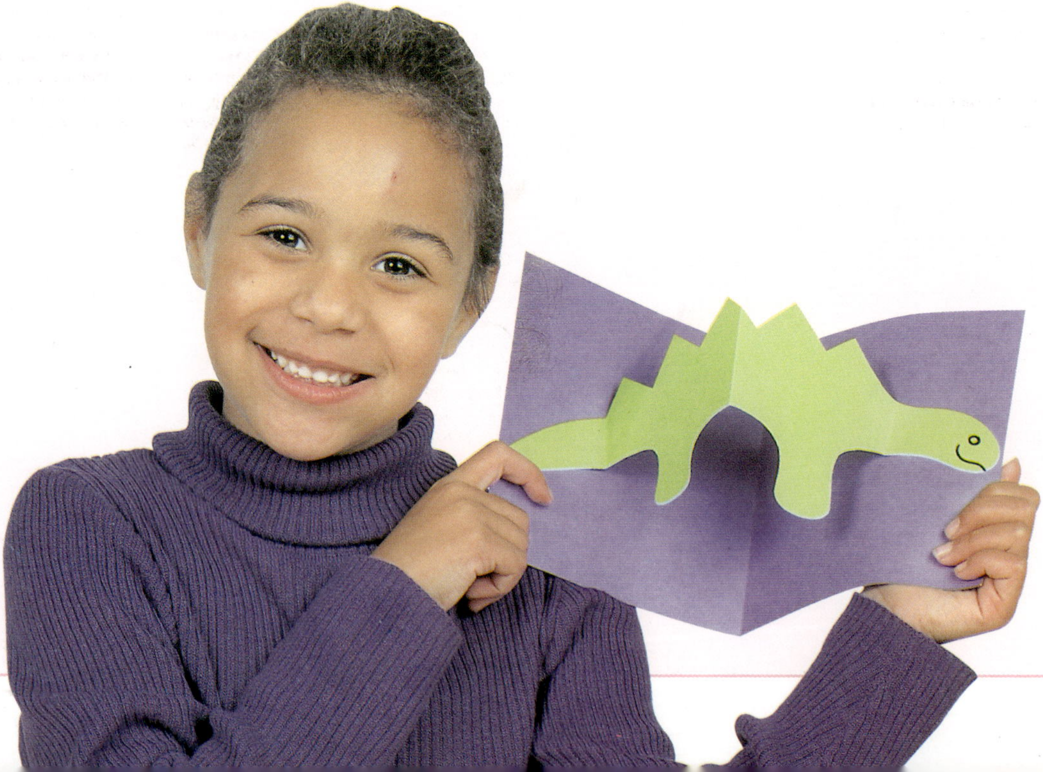